Star Guide

Other **Voyage into Space** Books

Saturn

Space Telescope

From Sputnik to Space Shuttles

Star Guide

Franklyn M. Branley
illustrated by Ellen Eagle

A **Voyage into Space** Book

Thomas Y. Crowell   New York

Photo credits: Mt. Wilson and Las Campanas Observatories,
Carnegie Institution of Washington, page 20; Science Graphics, page 14.

Star Guide

Library of Congress Cataloging-in-Publication Data
Branley, Franklyn Mansfield, 1915–
   Star guide.

   (A Voyage into space book)
   Includes index.
   Summary: Describes the composition and behavior of
stars and notes which ones can be seen at different
times of the year.
   1. Stars—Juvenile literature.   2. Astronomy—
Observers' manuals—Juvenile literature.   [1. Stars.
2. Astronomy—Observers' manuals]   I. Title.
II. Series.
QB801.7.B74 1987   523.8   82-45928
ISBN 0-690-04350-3
ISBN 0-690-04351-1 (lib. bdg.)

Designed by Al Cetta

1 2 3 4 5 6 7 8 9 10

First Edition

Contents

Star Guide

1. How Many Stars in the Universe?

The next time the night is dark and you are gazing at the sky, try counting the stars. It's hard to do, because you can't keep track of the ones already counted. If you could, you would find that you can see only two or three thousand. There are lots more, but they are very dim. We see only the brighter stars.

If you are on the ocean or high on a mountain, you'll see many more stars. That's because there is less dust in the air. Also, chances are the sky will be darker because you'll be away from the lights of cities and towns. You might be able to see four or five thousand stars.

If you use binoculars, you'll get a better view. Wherever you look, there will be lots of stars, half a million or more. There are more than you could count, even if you could keep track of them.

With a small telescope you can see two or three million stars. All of them belong to a large family of stars called the Milky Way galaxy. There are some 200 billion stars in the galaxy. One hundred billion is 1 followed by eleven zeros—

2

100,000,000,000. At the rate of one star a second, it would take 3,000 years to count 100 billion.

Astronomers have seen only a small number of the stars in our galaxy. Beyond the Milky Way, there are other galaxies, which together make up the universe. There must be billions of galaxies. And each one contains billions of stars. It would be impossible to count the number of stars in the universe.

In addition to the stars in our galaxy, there are gases. After a long time the gases may pack together and become stars. These gases and the stars make up more than 99 percent of all the material in the galaxy. All the planets, satellites, comets, and meteoroids are made of the small bit of material that is left over.

Stars are the main objects in our galaxy, and in the whole universe. So, let's find out what stars are, what they are made of, where they are and where they come from, how they move, and how they change.

The Milky Way galaxy is a spiral made of at least 200 billion stars. It is about 120,000 light-years across and 20,000 light-years from top to bottom at the thickest, central region. It rotates once in about 200 million years, taking us with it at a speed of about 160 miles per second. The solar system is located at X, some 32,000 light-years from the center of the galaxy.

2. The Sun and Its Neighbors

The sun is a star. It is the one that is nearest to us. Even though it's the closest star, the sun is a long way off. If you were in a spaceship traveling 25,000 miles an hour, it would take five months to get there. You would have to travel 93 million miles.

All the other stars are much farther away. They are so far that we see them only as points of light, even when using the biggest telescopes.

After the sun, the next nearest star is about 26 trillion miles away. Your spaceship would take more than 100,000 years to get there. The star is Alpha Centauri, in a group of stars called the constellation Centaurus. (A centaur is a mythological monster, half man and half horse.) When we look at Alpha Centauri, we see only one star. Actually, it is three stars that go around one another. At certain times, one of the three stars comes closer to Earth than the others ever do. That star is Proxima Centauri—proximity means closeness. Sometimes it is 4¼ light-years away.

Light-year

When astronomers measure big distances, they do not use miles. Instead, they use a light-year—it is the distance that light travels in one year. Light goes very fast, about 186,000 miles in one second. In one year it travels almost six trillion miles.

In one minute light goes about 11,000,000 miles. In 8⅓ minutes it goes about 93,000,000 miles, the distance to the sun. We can say that the distance to the sun is 8⅓ light-minutes.

The distance to Proxima Centauri is 4¼ light-years. It takes starlight that long to travel from Proxima Centauri to Earth.

Most stars are much farther away. In our galaxy some stars are 80,000 light-years from us. Some galaxies are

Light takes a bit more than eight minutes to travel to us from the sun. It takes about 4¼ light-years to travel to us from Proxima Centauri, the next nearest star.

8 light-minutes

The sky appears to be a bowl, with the stars all at the same distance and fixed to the inner surface. Actually, there is no "sky bowl," since the stars are located at various distances.

billions of light-years from the Milky Way. The farthest ones are about 10 billion light-years away. Light from them takes 10 billion years to reach us.

Stargazers of long ago did not know this. To them all the stars were the same distance away. They thought the sky was like the inside of a bowl turned upside down. The stars were fastened somehow to the bowl.

We can't blame them, for that's the way the sky appears. All the stars seem to be at the same distance from us. But they are not.

For example, the stars of Orion, the brightest of all the constellations, appear to be the same distance from us, arranged on a flat surface. They represent the hunter—his shoulders, knees, and belt.

If we could somehow travel to another location in the galaxy and look at the same stars, we would not see the hunter. We would then see that the stars are at different distances from Earth. The pattern of the hunter is seen only because of Earth's location.

Of the billions of stars in the universe, astronomers have studied only about 300,000. Most of them are nearby, well within the smallest circle in the drawing of the galaxy. Those stars are the ones we'll be talking about—our neighbor stars.

30,000
light-
years

2,000 light-years

Earth (the solar system)

5,000 light-years

10,000
light-
years

20,000
light-
years

50,000
light-
years

Most of the stars we observe are nearby in our galaxy, well within the smallest circle. Multitudes of additional stars lie at greater distances.

We see the constellations the way we do because of our location in the galaxy. If we could observe the stars from some other location, the familiar shapes of the constellations would not be apparent.

Hi- what's that?

It's my model of the constellation Orion!

It is? It doesn't look like Orion..

That's right! From where you are, it doesn't. But from here, it looks the way we know it !

TO PROXIMA CENTAURI

3. Dwarf Stars and Giants

All stars appear to be the same distance from us, and all except the sun appear as points of light. Some are brighter than others, and some may vary in color. But otherwise they appear alike. Actually, they are quite different. For example, many of the stars we see are really two stars going around each other. There may be three, four, or more, all going around one another. The sun may have a companion that is going around us, though no one has seen it, and not all astronomers agree about this.

The sun appears larger than a pinpoint only because it is close by. Many of the stars are much larger than the sun. Some are smaller.

The diameter of the sun, the distance across its center, is 864,000 miles—a bit less than one million. If the sun were a hollow ball, a million Earths would fit inside it. The volume of the sun is a million times Earth's volume.

Compared to Earth, the sun is huge. But some stars are much bigger.

Betelgeuse, a red star in Orion, is almost 500 million miles

The sun appears larger than the other stars because it is close by. Many of the stars are actually much larger than the sun. An apple that is three inches across can seem much larger than the sun, which is 864,000 miles across.

in diameter. It is so big that if it were the center of our solar system, the planets all the way out to Mars would be inside the star. Betelgeuse is a red supergiant.

But it is not the biggest star. Two of the biggest are Epsilon Aurigae and VV Cephei. (Epsilon Aurigae is part of the constellation Auriga, the charioteer, a northern constellation. VV Cephei is found in the constellation Cepheus, the king, which is in the far north next to Cassiopeia.) Epsilon Aurigae has a diameter of about one billion miles, and the diameter of VV Cephei is almost two billion miles. They are super-supergiants; billions of Earths would fit inside them.

Small stars are called dwarfs. The first one to be discovered was called the Pup. It is a companion of Sirius, the Dog Star. You can see Sirius in the winter skies. It is a bright

Betelgeuse

Sun

The Pup, a dwarf, would be about 1/30 this size.

The Earth would be about 1/120 this size.

A neutron star would be about 1/480,000 this size.

Stars vary in size—from black holes and neutron stars only a few miles across to VV Cephei, which may be two billion miles in diameter. The diameter of Earth is 8000 miles; that of the sun is 864,000 miles.

star, actually the brightest of all the stars we see, and it is in the constellation Canis Major, the great dog.

You cannot see the Pup; no one can. We know it is there because the Pup pulls on Sirius, causing it to move from side to side. It goes around Sirius once in about 50 years. Very likely it has a diameter of about 30,000 miles. You probably remember that the diameter of Earth is about 8,000 miles.

But there are smaller stars. One called Van Maanen's star has a diameter of only 6,000 miles. And one of the smallest, which has the number LP 768-500, has a diameter of only 1,000 miles. That makes it a lot smaller than the moon.

Volume and Density

The sun could contain a million Earths, meaning its size, or volume, is a million times the size of our planet.

The amount of matter in the sun adds up to only about 330,000 times the material in Earth. That means the matter in the sun, especially the outer part of it, is not packed

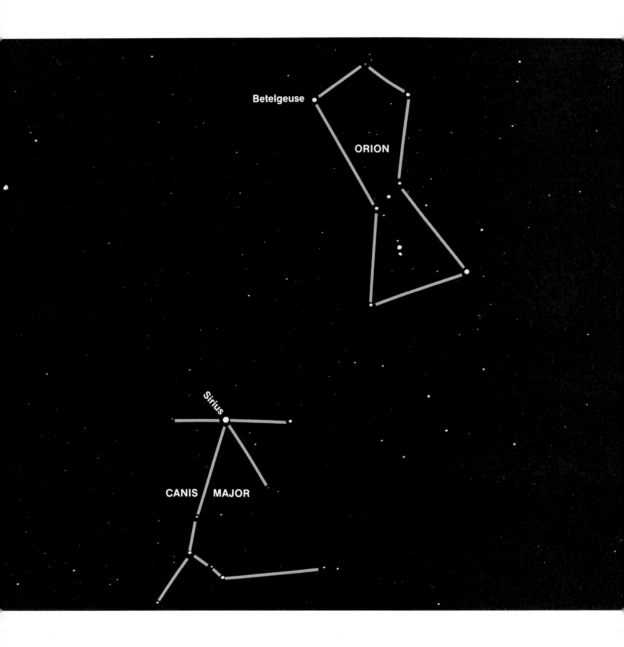

This section of the winter sky shows Sirius, the Dog Star, which is blue-white and the brightest of all the stars. Also notice Betelgeuse, a red supergiant that marks the right shoulder of Orion.

Density increases when more material is packed into the same space. In the nest on the left density is higher than it is in the nest on the right.

together as tightly as it is on Earth. The density of the sun is less than the density of Earth.

Volume is size: how big something is or how much it can hold. Density is quite different. It indicates how much matter something contains in a certain space, or how crowded it is. Suppose there are 30 children in a classroom. If 30 more children came into the classroom, the density would be twice as high. If there were only 15 children in the classroom, the density would be half as much.

Stars are made of gases. In some, the particles of gas are packed together tightly. The gas has a high density. Other

gases have a density that is much less than that of the sun. In supergiants like Betelgeuse and VV Cephie, the density is so low—the gas particles are spread so far apart—you could go right through them without even knowing it. A pint would weigh a fraction of an ounce.

The density of the air we breathe is 3,000 times greater than the density of supergiant stars.

In most dwarf stars the gases are packed together tightly. The density is very high. One pint of such a star could weigh 200 tons or more.

What Stars Are Made Of

Stars are made of the same materials, or elements, that we have here on Earth. About 60 different elements have been detected in the sun—elements such as iron, oxygen, hydrogen, gold, and sodium. About 90 percent of the sun is hydrogen, and almost 10 percent is helium. All the other elements, some 60 different ones, make up around 1 percent of the sun.

All the elements in the sun are in the form of gases. Indeed, all stars are made of gases. Sometimes the gases have little more substance than a shadow (the supergiants), and sometimes they are very dense (the dwarfs).

The Temperature of Stars

Whether density is high or low, the temperature of the gases is high. At the sun's surface, the temperature is 10,000 degrees Fahrenheit. That makes it medium hot. It is a yellow-orange star. The hotter a star is, the bluer it becomes. When you next look at Sirius, notice that it is blue-white. It is a very hot star, some 20,000 degrees. Some stars are much hotter.

Cool stars are reddish. The duller the color, the cooler they are. Betelgeuse is a red supergiant. Such stars have a temperature of about 5,000 degrees Fahrenheit. When the sky is clear, you should be able to see the redness of Betelgeuse.

The inside of stars is much hotter than the outside. Astronomers have not been able to measure temperature at the center of the sun, of course. But they can figure out what it is likely to be. It is probably 14 million degrees Fahrenheit at the center of the sun.

Stars provide the energy of the universe, just as the sun supplies Earth with its energy. Yet there is no oil or coal on the sun or on any of the other stars. There is no burning. Rather, the heat of the sun and other stars comes from nuclear reactions.

Gravity packs the gases in a star together. As the gases compact, the temperature goes up. When temperatures go very high, up to several million degrees, gases change from one kind to another. For example, hydrogen nuclei (the cores

of hydrogen atoms) join together to make helium nuclei. There is a nuclear reaction. When that happens, heat is released. Stars are huge nuclear furnaces that provide all the energy of the universe.

In some stars nuclear reactions occur rapidly. These stars are usually blue-white giants, and they last for only a few million years.

In other stars, such as the reddish ones, the reactions occur more slowly. These stars may last for 20 billion years or so, longer than the 10-billion-year life span of the sun.

4. Lifetimes of Stars

Stars do not last forever. They may lose gases, or collapse, or blow up. Nuclear reactions may slow, and then the star cools down. Stars disappear, and new ones are born.

Gases abound in the space between stars, in interstellar space, as it is called. The gases may have been there for billions of years, and more gases may have been added as stars exploded. There is more than enough gas in interstellar space to make millions of stars.

When the gases collect together, they form a nebula, which is often bright enough for astronomers to see.

Dark spots may be detected in these nebulas. These are places where the gases are packing together because of gravity. More and more gases collect. As they pack together, the temperature of the gases increases. After a long time,

Nebulas, such as this one in Monoceros, the unicorn, just east of Orion, are large formations of gases. Dark patches are where the gases have become concentrated. The gases pack together, collapse, and become new stars. Smaller masses may become planets.

millions or even billions of years, the gases become so hot that nuclear reactions begin. A new star is born.

If there is not much matter in the new star and the density is low, the star will be a dim, feeble object. If there is a lot of matter and density is high, the star will be hot and bright.

A low-density star may shine for a hundred billion years.

Stars that are cool are usually dim, and hot stars are usually bright. When charted, most of them fall somewhere along the curved region in the diagram. It is called the Hertzsprung-Russell diagram after the two astronomers who first assembled and organized the information.

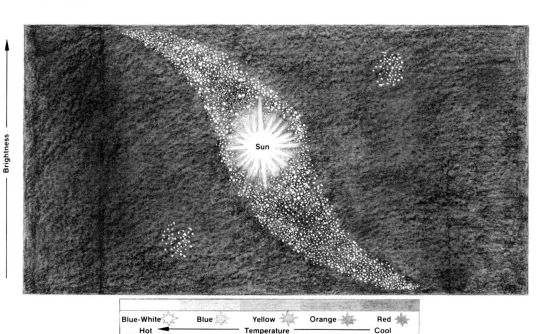

On the other hand, hot, bright stars don't last long. They burn out in only a few million years. Inside temperatures may soar so high that the star is blown apart. A large part of the star is blown into space. As this happens, for a short time the star becomes much brighter—it is a nova or "new" star. If the star is very bright, the star is a supernova.

Gravitation is now greater than the force pushing outward, and so the core of a supernova may pack tighter and tighter. Density becomes very high. A teaspoon of such a star might weigh a million tons.

Atoms could not exist inside a star having this density. Only cores of the atoms would remain, the neutrons. The once brilliant star would become a neutron star.

It would give off radio pulses. We would know it existed

Atoms shown on the left cannot fit together tightly because of the electron fields around the nuclei. In a neutron star, the electron fields break down. Therefore the nuclei of the atoms—the neutrons—can pack closely together. More nuclei can pack into the same space, so density becomes very high.

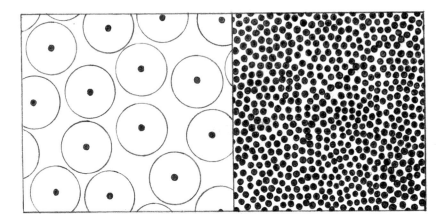

because our radio telescopes would pick up those pulses. It would be a pulsar, a pulsating neutron star.

Should the star pack even tighter, it would become a black hole. That's what may happen to stars that are several times more massive than the sun. Less massive stars become dwarfs.

A black hole has very strong gravity. Earth has gravity, of course. In order to escape from Earth, a spaceship (or an atom or anything else) must go 7 miles a second to overcome the force of gravity. That is Earth's escape velocity.

Because a black hole has tremendous gravity, the escape velocity from one is greater than 186,000 miles a second—the speed of light. Nothing can go that fast, so nothing can escape from a black hole—not X rays, radio waves, or light. That's why it is called a black hole—we cannot see it.

We know it is there because of X rays. Black holes usually have ordinary stars as companions. They pull gases out of the companion star. Just before the gases speed into the black hole, they release X rays. Wherever astronomers see a steady stream of X rays near a bright star, they suspect there is a black hole. One of the first to be discovered was Cygnus X-1. It is in the neck of Cygnus, the swan, found in the summer skies.

A black hole existing as a companion of a large, bright star. Gases are pulled into the black hole, emitting X rays as they go "over the edge."

Stars change, they come and go. In your lifetime you probably won't see changes in the appearance of the stars. But during your lifetime new stars will be created, and old stars will go out of existence. Because they may be thousands of light-years away, we'll know about those changes only after thousands of years have gone by.

All the stars in our galaxy are changing, and they are traveling their separate ways. So are all the stars in all the galaxies that make up the universe.

5. Motions of Stars

Stars seem to rise and set, as does the sun. Every night they appear to journey across the sky. The motion is an illusion that occurs only because Earth is rotating. As Earth turns toward the east, stars appear to rise in the east. At the same time we turn away from the stars in the west—they seem to set.

Stars rise and set and journey across the sky, but they do not seem to change position relative to one another. For example, Betelgeuse will remain the shoulder star of Orion throughout our lifetimes. As long as we look at the stars in the Big Dipper they will be in the same positions where we now see them. But we don't look at them very long—a human lifetime is short. Thousands of years from now people will not see the Dipper as we see it today. That's because the stars in the Dipper, and all the other stars as well, are moving.

Astronomers know the directions stars are moving, and their speeds. The motions of a few stars are shown in the drawing—the longer the arrow, the faster the speed.

Because of these motions, the appearance of the Dipper

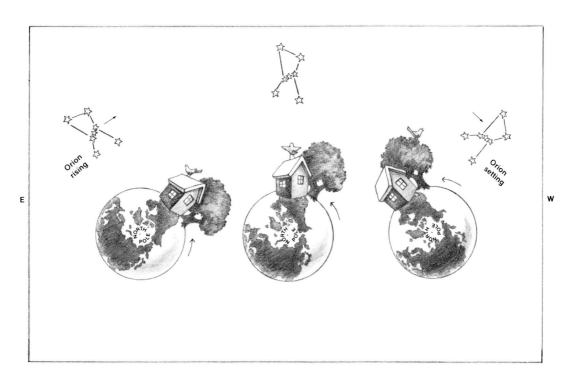

The stars seem to rise, moving higher in the sky and westward.
Then they appear lower in the sky and set in the west. The apparent
motion occurs because Earth is moving in the opposite direction,
that is, from west to east.

50,000 years ago

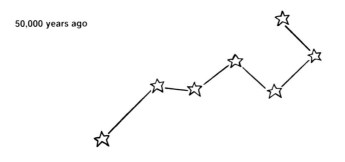

Today

50,000 years from now

Each star has its own motion. Because of their great distances, the motions are not apparent to us. However, delicate instruments measure the motions, revealing that the stars of the Big Dipper are moving, as shown by the arrows. Fifty thousand years from now the Dipper will be much flatter. (Length of arrows indicates relative velocity.)

changes. Fifty thousand years ago the bowl of the Dipper was quite square. And 50,000 years from now the bowl will be much flatter than it is now.

The sun is also moving through space. As it moves, the sun carries Earth and the entire solar system with it. We are speeding through space at 45,000 miles an hour toward the constellation Hercules. We are aware of the motion only when we measure it against the motion of other stars. The only star motion apparent to us is the one from east to west, which results from Earth's rotation.

We also notice changes in the stars from season to season. This is because we revolve around the sun, and so our nighttime view of the sky changes.

6. Stars Through the Year

If you faced south and gazed at the sky, the stars seen throughout the year would pass by you in 24 hours. You would be able to see only some of them, of course, because during part of those 24 hours there would be daylight.

A belt of star patterns all around the sky is shown in the illustration. These are the constellations of the zodiac, as well as those that are close to the zodiac. The center line of the zodiac is the ecliptic, the path the sun follows during a year. As you can see by reading the months, the sun moves from west to east. The straight line is the celestial equator, which divides the sphere of the sky into northern and southern halves.

There are 12 constellations in the zodiac. In the entire sky there are 88 constellations that are recognized by astronomers. Most of us find it difficult to identify a good many of them because they are dim, and they have no distinctive shape. However, it is quite easy to identify three or four during each of the seasons by following these few directions and using our diagrams to guide you.

Our time for viewing will be 9:00 P.M. standard time—that

During a year the sun moves along the ecliptic eastward. We see stars that are opposite the sun's location. For example, in summer we see Sagittarius; the sun is in Gemini. The twelve zodiacal constellations through which the sun moves are shown with darker lines.

will be one hour later when you are using daylight saving time. Also, we'll be looking toward the south.

The diagrams are for the middle of the month. Should you be stargazing earlier in the month, or earlier than 9:00, the stars will appear farther to the east, your left, as you look south. Later in the month, or later at night, the entire sky will appear farther to the west, or your right. The zenith (overhead) and horizon are about 40 degrees north latitude. But wherever you are in the United States, they will be about as shown.

Winter Skies

In the winter months, Orion is the outstanding constellation. You should have no trouble seeing it because of the bright stars it contains. On clear, dark nights you'll see that Betelgeuse is a red star. Rigel, directly opposite, is blue-white.

The brightest star in the area is Sirius. It is in Canis Major and is the brightest star in the entire sky.

Above Orion and a bit to the right is Aldebaran, another bright star. It is the eye of Taurus, the bull. Notice Taurus is in a V formation. By extending the arms of the V you reach two stars that are the tips of the bull's horns.

Connect the belt stars of Orion—Alnilam, Alnitak, and Mintaka—to make a line. Continue the line and it takes you to Aldebaran. A bit beyond is a cluster of stars called the Pleiades. It makes the shoulder of Taurus.

Notice that the ecliptic goes through Taurus. During summer, the sun is in this part of the sky.

Just below Orion is Lepus, the hare. All the stars in it are quite dim. Just above Orion and to the left are Castor and Pollux, two rather bright stars that mark the constellation Gemini, the twins.

Eridanus, the river, is a wandering constellation that covers a large segment of the sky. All the stars in it are dim, and so chances are you will have a hard time tracing out the entire group.

High in the sky you should see Capella, another of the bright stars. It is in the constellation Auriga, the charioteer. Sometimes it is called the goat, and the dim stars alongside are called the kids.

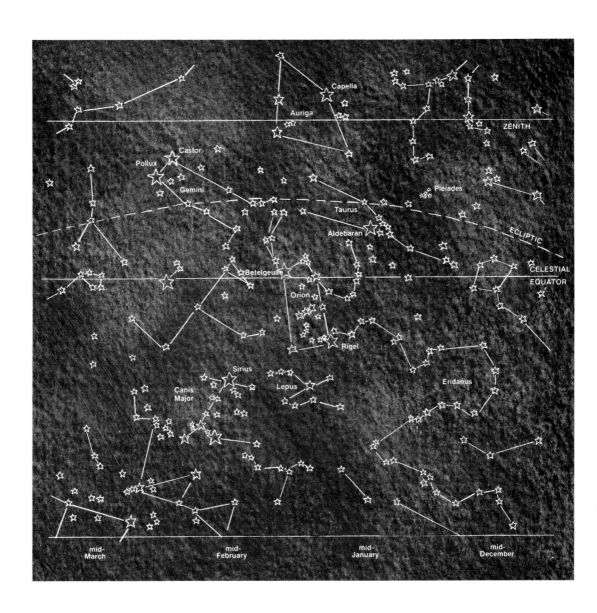

Capella

Auriga

ZENITH

Castor

Pollux

Gemini

Pleiades

Taurus

ECLIPTIC

Aldebaran

CELESTIAL
EQUATOR

Betelgeuse

Orion

Rigel

Sirius

Lepus

Eridanus

Canis
Major

mid-
March

mid-
February

mid-
January

mid-
December

TO PROXIMA CENTAURI

Spring Skies

As we move toward the warmer days of April, the springtime stars take over the sky. Leo, the lion, is fairly easy to identify. The head of the lion is shaped like a sickle, with Regulus, the brightest star in the region, marking the handle. East of Regulus (your left) is a triangle of stars that marks the hindquarters. The principal star in the triangle is Denebola.

Below Leo are four stars forming an uneven rectangle. They also mark the constellation Corvus, the crow. It looks more like a sail than a crow. It is just above the horizon. The dim stars just to the right are the constellations Crater and Hydra, neither of which is outstanding. Just west of Regulus, to the right, you may be able to see a small cluster of stars: the head of Hydra, the sea serpent.

The bright star to the east (your left) is Spica, in the constellation Virgo, the maiden.

Notice that the ecliptic crosses the celestial equator just below Denebola. The intersection is called the autumnal equinox. In autumn the sun is at this location—the start of the fall season.

The constellation Antlia, the air pump, and a portion of Vela, the sail, are dim. Also, chances are they will be too close to the horizon for you to detect.

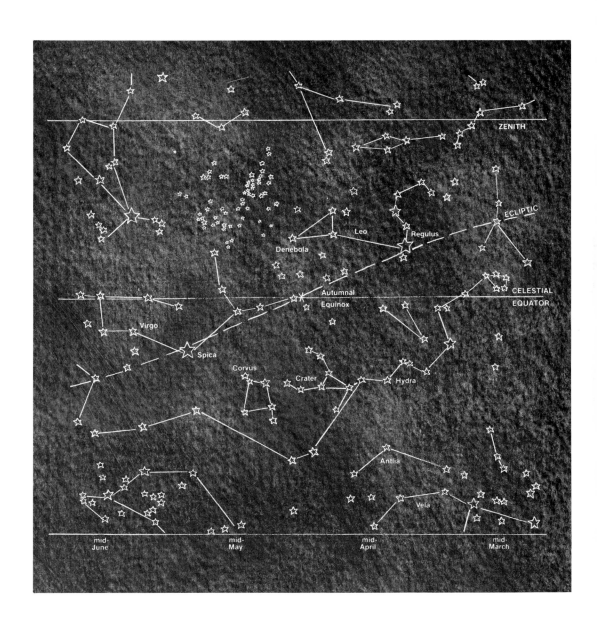

ZENITH

ECLIPTIC

Leo
Denebola
Regulus

Autumnal
Equinox

CELESTIAL
EQUATOR

Virgo

Spica

Corvus

Crater

Hydra

Antlia

Vela

mid-
June

mid-
May

mid-
April

mid-
March

TO PROXIMA CENTAURI

Summer Skies

In mid-August you'll be able to see Sagittarius, the archer, low in the southern sky. It is supposed to represent a drawn bow and an arrow ready to be released. It is often called the teapot, and you can see why—the pot, handle and lid and spout, are all quite apparent. If you continue straight up from Sagittarius to the zenith, you'll come to Vega, a very bright star in the constellation Lyra, the lyre.

West of the teapot (your right) is Scorpius, with the bright red star Antares, called the rival of Mars because its color is much like that of the red planet.

Above Antares is Ophiuchus, the serpent bearer. You may be able to identify the fairly bright star Sabik, just above Antares and a bit to the left. The rest of the constellation is hard to see except under very good conditions.

Not so with Altair, to the east. It is a bright star identified by the dim stars on either side of it. The star is the clue to finding Aquila, the eagle. Don't worry if you find it hard to see an eagle.

Above Altair is the constellation Cygnus, the swan. You could think of it as a swan with outstretched wings. Its tail would be the bright star Deneb, and its head Albireo. The star group is often called the Northern Cross, the upright extending from Deneb to Albireo, and the wings of the swan being the arms of the cross.

Notice that the ecliptic dips well below the celestial equator. Winter begins when the sun is at the lowest point of the ecliptic; that would be in Sagittarius.

During summer, the Milky Way can be seen the most clearly of any time of the year. That's because we are looking toward the center of the galaxy, where star numbers are greatest. Should you be lucky enough to have a clear, dark sky, such as at the seashore or on a mountaintop, the formation will be quite apparent.

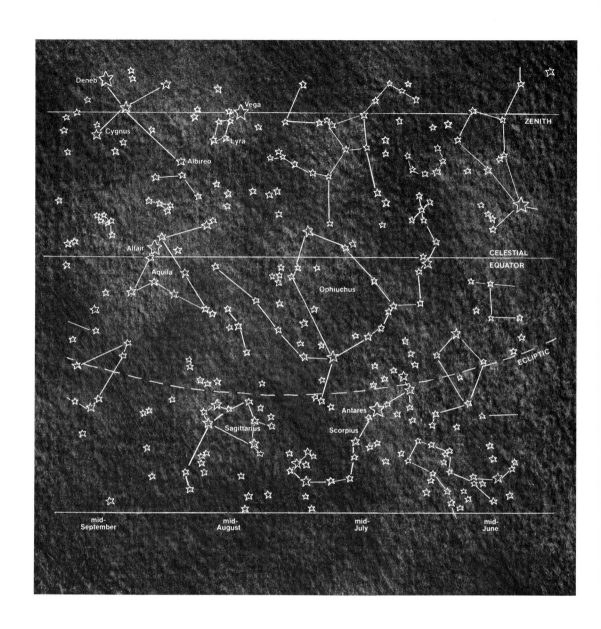

Deneb

Vega

Cygnus

Lyra

Albireo

ZENITH

Altair

CELESTIAL

EQUATOR

Aquila

Ophiuchus

ECLIPTIC

Antares

Sagittarius

Scorpius

mid-
September

mid-
August

mid-
July

mid-
June

TO PROXIMA CENTAURI

Autumn Skies

The skies of the fall season are readily identified by the presence of the great square of Pegasus, the flying horse. It is usually represented as half of an upside-down horse, with Enif marking its nose. The stars radiating from Scheat show its forelegs.

Alpheratz, the upper and eastern star of the square, is shared with the constellation Andromeda, the princess. Mirach and Almach, two other stars in Andromeda, extend eastward from Alpheratz. Just above Mirach is M31, the Andromeda galaxy, which can be detected with binoculars as a blur.

East of Pegasus (your left) is a group of stars marking the head of the northern fish, and below Pegasus is the head of the western fish. The bodies extend south and east, enmeshing where they meet. The constellation is Pisces, the fishes.

If you were to draw a line from Alpheratz to Algenib and extend the line southward from Algenib the same distance, you would be close to the intersection of the ecliptic and the celestial equator. This is the vernal equinox, the sun's location on the first day of spring.

Cetus, the whale, is rather dim except for Deneb Kaitos, a bright star that is on your meridian (a line passing overhead from the north pole to the south pole) in mid-November. It is a large constellation, and one that contains Mira, the wonderful. It is a variable star that varies in brightness regularly. It was known to the ancients, for it disappeared and reappeared every 332 days, and it still does.

Sculptor and Phoenix are hard to detect because they are far to the south and dim.

Even though it is low in the sky, you may be able to see Fomalhaut because it is a bright star. It is in the constellation Piscis Austrinus, the southern fish.

The ecliptic runs through Aquarius, the water carrier. As centuries go by, the vernal equinox moves westward along the ecliptic because of a shift in the direction of Earth's axis. This means that a few centuries from now the sun will be in Aquarius on the first day of spring. Also, Polaris will not be directly above Earth's north pole.

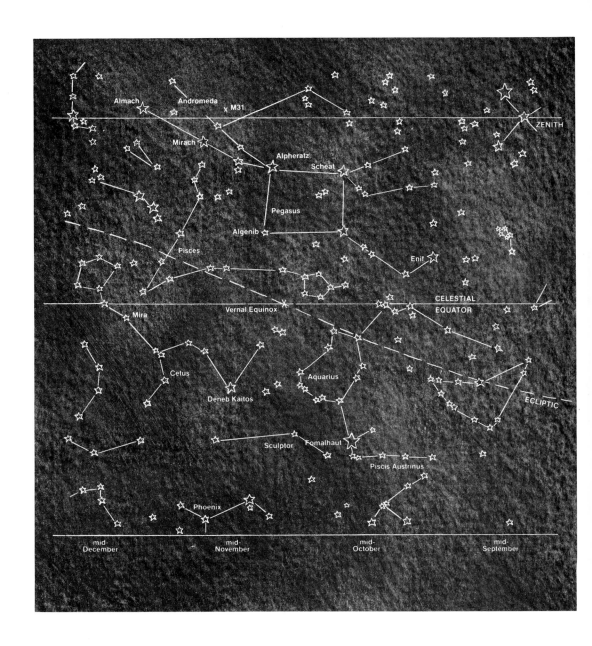

Almach
Andromeda
χ M31
ZENITH
Mirach
Alpheratz
Scheat
Pegasus
Algenib
Enif
Pisces
CELESTIAL
Vernal Equinox
EQUATOR
Mira
ECLIPTIC
Cetus
Aquarius
Deneb Kaitos
Sculptor
Fomalhaut
Piscis Austrinus
Phoenix

mid-December   mid-November   mid-October   mid-September

TO PROXIMA CENTAURI

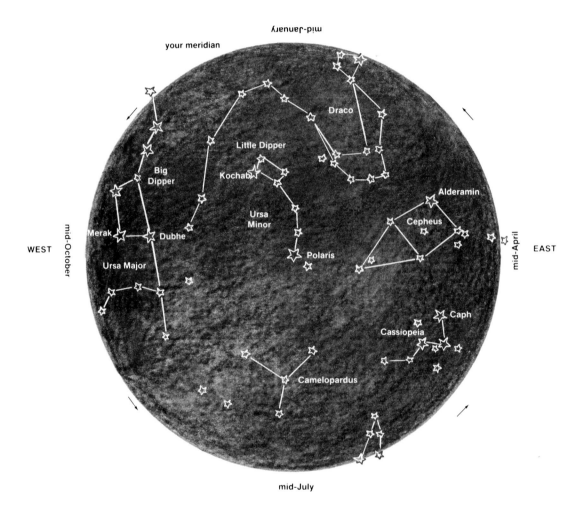

The Polar Sky

Because of Earth's rotation, the entire sky seems to wheel around Polaris, the north star, making one complete turn in 24 hours. Because of your location, which we assume is around 40 degrees north latitude, the stars shown in the diagram do not rise and set. (The elevation of Polaris above the horizon is equal to your latitude. As seen from the equator, which is zero degrees latitude, Polaris is on the horizon; from the north pole, Polaris is at 90 degrees—directly overhead.)

If you look northward at 9:00 P.M. in mid-July, the sky will be as shown in the diagram. The entire sky appears to turn counterclockwise around Polaris. Therefore, later at night, the Big Dipper will be closer to the horizon.

The Dipper is standing on the end of the bowl. Merak and Dubhe, called the pointer stars, direct you toward Polaris. Extend a line from them that is about five times the distance between the two stars. It takes you very near Polaris. The Dipper is not a constellation; it is a small part of Ursa Major, the great bear.

Polaris is the first star in the handle of the Little Dipper, which appears to be emptying into the Big Dipper. (This dipper is not a constellation either; it is part of Ursa Minor, the little bear.) Polaris is not a bright star, and it is located some 780 light-years from us. We see it as it was 780 years ago. The fairly bright star Kochab may help you locate the bowl of the Little Dipper.

If you continue the line connecting Dubhe and Polaris, you come to Cepheus, the king. Most people see the constellation more as a lopsided house than the figure of a person. The brightest star in the region is Alderamin, though it is not outstanding, being a bit dimmer than Polaris. Because of an

Earth motion called precession, the north pole of Earth is not always directly under Polaris. About 5,000 years from now it will be more nearly under Alderamin. In other words, Alderamin will then be our north star.

Alongside Cepheus is Cassiopeia, the queen, or the queen's chair, as it is often called. In mid-July it appears to be an uneven letter W, with Caph the uppermost star—a bit dimmer than Polaris. Six months later it will appear more like an M.

About halfway between Polaris and the horizon is Camelopardis, the camel-leopard or giraffe. The stars in it are all dim, and in no way does the configuration remind one of a giraffe. Don't despair if you have trouble detecting it.

Between Polaris and the star Vega is Draco, the dragon. It is another of the constellations of dim stars. However, on clear nights you may be able to detect the stars snaking across the sky between the Dippers, and also extending to the region between Polaris and Cepheus.

As the year goes by, the polar sky at 9:00 P.M. will change. About three months later, in mid-October, the Big Dipper will be on the horizon. (Turn the diagram so that mid-October is on the bottom.) Chances are you'll be able to see only part of the Dipper.

By mid-January at 9:00 P.M. the Dipper can be seen clearly, standing on its handle. In the springtime the Dipper will be upside down, emptying into the Little Dipper.

Wherever you go on Earth, and whenever, you can get a lot of pleasure from finding familiar stars and constellations and discovering ones you haven't known before. And you need no equipment—just your eyes and curiosity. In the next year we hope you'll be able to find the stars and constellations we have mentioned here, and maybe eventually you'll see and recognize all 88 constellations. That's something not too many people have accomplished.

If the rocket keeps going at the rate
of 140 light-minutes per page, it
will take 249 more books of this length
before it reaches Proxima Centauri,
the next-closest star to Earth
after the sun.

Further Reading

Branley, Franklyn M. *Black Holes, White Dwarfs, and Super-stars*. New York: Thomas Y. Crowell, 1976.

_____. *The Sun: Star Number One*. New York: Thomas Y. Crowell, 1964.

Chartrand, Mark R. *The Sky Guide*. New York: Western Publishing Company, 1982.

Polgreen, John and Cathleen. *The Stars Tonight*. New York: Harper & Row, 1967.

Index

Spica, 34, *35*
spring:
    sky chart, 34, *35*
    sun's location in, 38
stargazing diagrams, 30-42
stars:
    birth of, 19-21, *20*
    brightness of, *14*, 21, *21*
    color of, 17, *21*
    composition of, 16
    density of, 13-16
    distances from Earth, 4-7, *5, 6, 8*
    lifetimes of, 18, 19-25
    motions of, 26-29, *27, 28*
    new, 21-22
    number of, 1-3
    sizes of, 10-15, *11, 12*
    temperature of, 17-18, 21-22, *21*
summer:
    sky chart, 36, *37*
    sun's location in, 32
sun:
    density of, 13-15
    diameter of, 10, *12, 13*
    distance from Earth, 4, 5, *11*
    elements found in, 16
    life span of, 18
    location on ecliptic, *31*
    motion of, 29
    size of, 10-11, *11, 12*, 13
    temperature of, 17
supergiants, 10-11, 16
supernova, 22
super-supergiants, 11
swan (Cygnus), 23, *31*, 36, *37*

Taurus, *31*, 32, *33*
teapot (Sagittarius), *31*, 36, *37*

telescope, stars seen with, 1
temperature:
    of stars, 17-18, *21*, 21-22
    of sun, 17
Triangulum, *31*
twins (Gemini), *31*, 32, *33*

unicorn (Monoceros), *20*
universe, 3, 24
Ursa Major, *40*, 41
Ursa Minor, *40*, 41

Van Maanen's star, 13
variable stars, 38
Vega, 36, *37*
Vela, 34, *35*
vernal equinox, 38, *39*
Virgo, *31*, 34, *35*
visibility of stars, 1-2
volume, defined, 15
VV Cephei, 11, *12*, 16

watercarrier (Aquarius), *31*, 38, *39*
whale (Cetus), *31*, 38, *39*
winter:
    sky charts, *14*, 32, *33*
    sun's location in, 37
wonderful (Mira), 38, *39*

X rays, 23, *24*

yellow-orange stars, 17

zodiac, constellations of, 30-31, *31*

Franklyn M. Branley, Astronomer Emeritus and former Chairman of The American Museum–Hayden Planetarium, is well known as the author of many popular books about astronomy and other sciences for young people of all ages. He is also the originator of the Let's-Read-and-Find-Out Science Book series.